AF605259

One Race

Gregg Dreise

A Scholastic Press book from Scholastic Australia

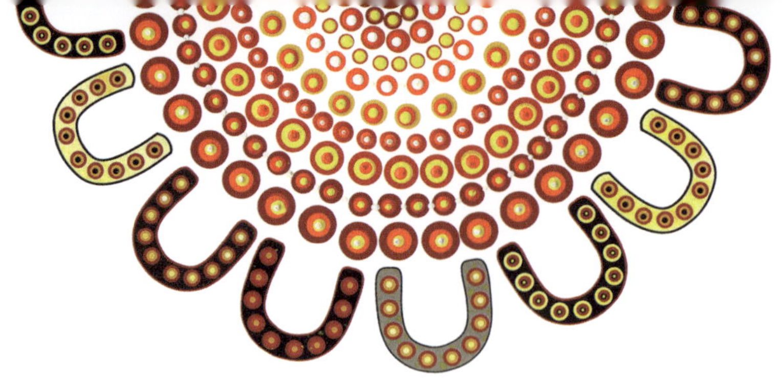

This book is dedicated to all of the beautiful people who embrace colour and humanity. Your wonderful respect and kindness makes the world a better place for us all. G.D.

Scholastic Press
An imprint of Scholastic Australia Pty Limited (ABN 11 000 614 577)
PO Box 579 Gosford NSW 2250
www.scholastic.com.au

Part of the Scholastic Group
Sydney • Auckland • New York • Toronto • London • Mexico City
New Delhi • Hong Kong • Buenos Aires • Puerto Rico

Published by Scholastic Australia in 2026.

A catalogue record for this book is available from the National Library of Australia

ISBN: 978-1-76129-858-5

Typeset in IM FELL DW PICA.
Book design by Hannah Janzen.

Gregg Dreise created the artwork in this book with black pen, black permanent markers, watercolours and acrylic paint.

We acknowledge the Traditional Owners of the Country on which we live and work. We pay respect to Elders past and present.

Printed in China by RR Donnelley.

Scholastic Australia's policy, in association with RR Donnelley, is to use papers that are renewable and made efficiently with wood from responsibly managed sources, so as to minimise its environmental footprint.

10 9 8 7 6 5 4 3 2 1 26 27 28 29 30 / 2

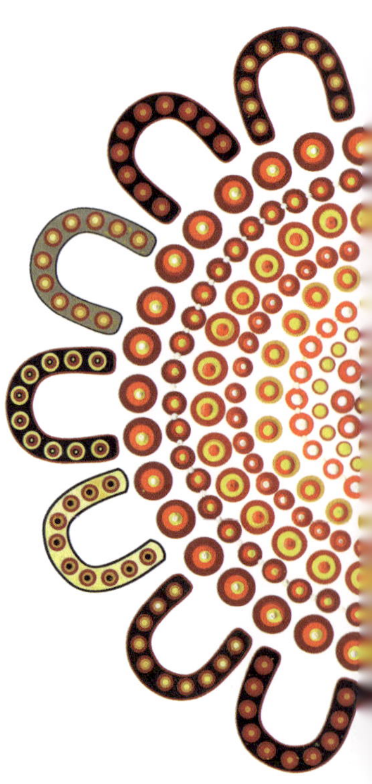

How can there be **racism**

when we are **one** human race?

Our difference

is our biggest **strength;**

not something to debase.

We are **unique**

and we are **many**,

joined regardless

of birth place.

Walking side-by-side
as human beings

is what we should embrace.

H
M
U
A

How can our **humanity**

be something we misplace?

UNITY

It is the soul of **unity**;

it should be our solid base.

Instead of seeking status
that we are brainwashed
to chase.

We need to help each other

to climb up this life's staircase.

Kindness and compassion
build communities of grace.

Yet there are still some people

who throw out **awful** words

like mace.

Let's communicate with empathy;
not get all up in your face.

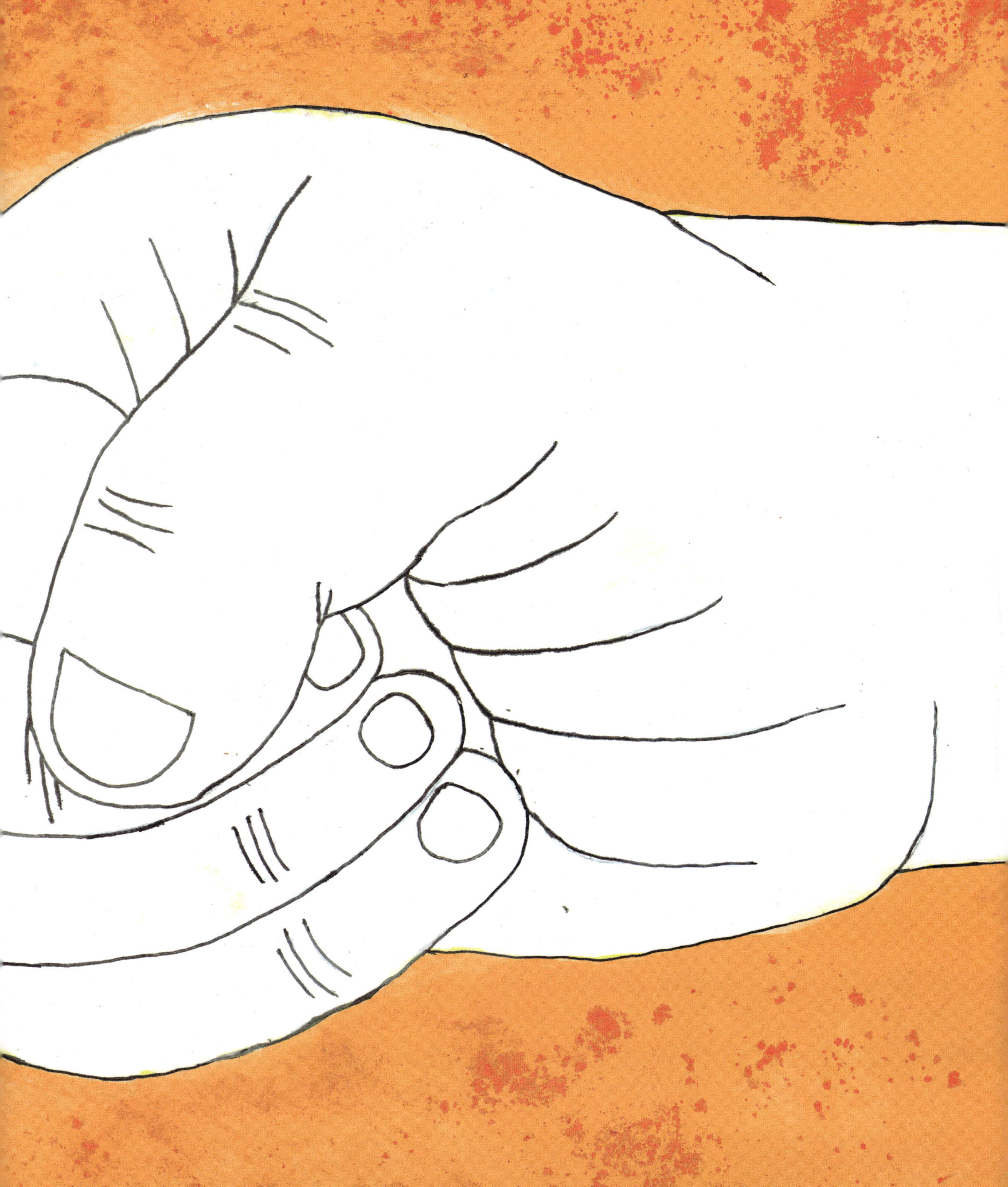

And build a life

where we walk with **harmony**

as our common-place.

How can there be racism,

when there is only **you** and **me**?

I'm **positive** that we understand;

so, I'm making this **plea**.

Being proud of our

unique differences,

now that is the **key**.

There wouldn't;

shouldn't;

couldn't
be racism . . .

. . . if humanity moves
forward with equality.